AT RISK

AT RISK

Poems

~

Teresa Cader

Winner of the 2023
Richard Snyder Memorial Publication Prize
Selected by Mark Doty

THE ASHLAND POETRY PRESS

Printed in the United States of America

ISBN: 978-1-964957-00-5

LCCN: 2024940527

Author Photo: Jerry Mechling

Cover art: "Białe Szczyty" by Olga Pawłowska, by permission

Cover design: Nicholas Fedorchak, Mike Ruhe

Editor: Chuck Carlise

For Jerry

and in memory of my father
Tadeusz Józef Cader
1913-2007

Poetry books by Teresa Cader

Guests
The Paper Wasp
History of Hurricanes

CONTENTS

I

II POLAND: A FUGUE

I

AT RISK

The hunting dog, beaten silly for missing pheasants
when he lost their scent in the mist over the meadow,

tied to a fence post all night in the field where mosquitoes
swarmed his ears,

hides behind his rescue family on the Long Pond Path in the Fells.

They say *It's okay, Dave.*
To us: *He's afraid of people,*
but he loves other dogs.

Dave doesn't bark; our old dog wouldn't bark
once frail, mostly deaf and going blind—
safer to hide in silence.

~

Two police cars front the house across from the Scranton Diner,
where we eat a turkey club and coleslaw,
talk about the fear in Dave's eyes

and his sleek brown and black coat, his pointer tail, and the love
his owners show him.

Nice anniversary, so far, we say, pleased with our hike and the diner
which reminds us of our small-town roots.

What happened? we ask the waitress, looking at the police cars.

Overdose, she says. *He was stone cold dead when his mother found him.*

~

On oxycontin after surgery,
I answered the phone:
This is Alice in Wonderland,
and all I'm wearing is a pinafore.

A man said *Hello, what?* and hung up.
I crawled back to bed, reattaching
the ice machine to my purple and gold shoulder,
strapping myself to the bed.

I needed another dose, the pain tore into my bones deeper
from moving, from breathing too fast.

When my husband called from his conference, the phone rang
as I watched the red light blink
like an airport runway signal.

~

The police corner a young man who props himself against
a telephone pole, his pale freckled skin
flushed like he has a fever.

The mother ran in here to call 911, our waitress announces,
We know them all, even the son.

We look back to the street and a policeman leans into a car.
A woman is slumped
over the steering wheel.

The waitress tells us: *That's the mother.*

~

We should rescue a dog, my husband says,
as we walk past the young man the police
still question,
and the mother who lifts her head,
and stares at them.

A rescue dog just mauled a child, I respond,
they can be very damaged.

Damage can get into the brain, hopeless
to try to erase it.

We don't have kids at home anymore, my husband says.
You're afraid to take a risk.

I am, I say, as I watch a crowd gather on the sidewalk
to wait for the stretcher.

JUNK MOON

The gun still, the mask black, his amber eyes
scared
beneath a black tasseled beanie pulled low.

I heard my voice shake snow from the boughs
of firs,
the silent houses watching my head hit ground.

Where has he gone, the clever teen who chose
to mug
a woman when deep snow muted his footsteps,

finding an unplowed street in Cambridge at dusk,
the trucks
still circling the Square, shovels stowed in doorways.

Sometimes in a snowstorm the moon appears,
sliced
like cantaloupe on a white plate.

I'd wanted to escape a phone that wouldn't ring
with apologies,
to tame my mind by foraging in the starkness

of sidewalks, fences, tire tracks disappearing,
to glimpse
a sliver of orange moonlight through wind gusts.

I've studied the origins of the moon since then—
massive debris
from earth's collision with Theia, the size of Mars.

No bloodied eclipse, no Harvest, no Blue or orange,
sees me
walk alone beneath the scrapyard of a junk moon.

Where has he put *his* memory of that snowstorm,
my face,
or the lucky indifference of the well-lit houses?

SEA OTTERS, MISSILES, SARDINES

Monterey Bay, March 2022

Sea otters sun themselves on harbor rocks,
then dive
for mussels, lunch on their backs near kayaks,

while sails snap, a houseboat pivots, gulls shriek.
On my iPhone
patrols forage in rubble after a missile explodes

in the city whose name sticks on my tongue
the way
Buczkowice once did, my father's Polish village,

where Nazi artillery hit our family house, missed
the porch
where he played in "The War to End All Wars."

In canneries here in 1916, at all hours of the night,
immigrant men
unloaded nets of sardines and women sorted them,

standing for twelve hours in frigid bloody water,
feeding Europe's
craze for those *silver synchronized swimmers,*

eaten with mustard, or tomatoes and white onions,
named for
the prized fish of fifteenth-century Sardinia.

A swimmer floats near seals, pulled by the current,
no wet suit,
and the sun glazes the cold white-capped waves.

Two sea otters hold paws in the shallows, splash,
playful as Max,
Steinbeck's dog who ate a draft of *East of Eden*.

He called the canneries *a poem, a stink, a grating noise,*
unlike the pitch-
drop music my daughter makes reading to me in Japanese.

She says an Ainu myth blames human imperfection
on a sea otter,
who went fishing instead of finishing God's work.

THOUGHTS AND PRAYERS

Sometimes when the news pours into the kitchen,
chairs sway like circus elephants—

live shooter in an elementary school—

I go under my tent that collapses into darkness,
half-smothering the children inside me.

To save them I hold my chair to the floor,
my feet to the ground,

and say, *I'll keep you safe.*
I turn off the news, open the tent flap,

see a woman walking a miniature poodle,
teens jogging in blue shorts.

Slowly the children crawl toward the light,
my green eyes where theirs should be.

I am the mother who can't lift the car,
not the one who defied the odds.

I play jazz on the radio, make soup, try to ease
them back into their sunny play,

where the sweet island of my kitchen
could make the dead bodies not our own,

wrong as that might be.

A GARDEN AND A STREET

Where in my body do I feel peace, the meditation leader wants to know,
and I scan my mind trying to remember the Japanese white stone garden

raked in concentric circles around smooth dark boulders, no human footprint
visible, as if some spirit had descended from the sky to rake before dawn.

Instead, I see a street of rubble from bombed-out buildings, jagged hunks
of concrete blocking the way, bits of bloodied cloth snagged on top like flags.

Can I use my breath to unclench my mind, returning to the white stones,
letting go of fear and my attachment to the suffering of the world, he asks,

and I say I don't know. If I find peace in the white stones of the garden,
but don't clean up the rubble of the street, what good is my mind?

THE BATTLE OF MENOTOMY

West Cambridge

When I saunter to the mailbox in miserable sun,
a woman stares at the stone marker by my fence—

Site of the house of John Cutter set on fire
during the British retreat of April 19, 1775

Dogs piss on it. A traffic box cautions
walkers at the crosswalk: *wait, wait, wait.*

Ambushed by 4,000 militia, the Brits torched
houses and barns during the day's bloodiest fight,

royal bayonets gutting Jason and his friends
at the Jason Russell House across the street.

In third grade I fell in love with glossy books
about the founding fathers, the women in bonnets

churning butter in barrels, that righteous hunger.
What did I know of myths and facts? The Russells

and their kind owned *servants*, some diaries say.
Now our town fights over low-income housing.

Jazz on the Russell House lawn, pop-up beer
gardens in tents, the annual battle reenactments…

Nearby in the Old Burying Ground, unmarked
graves of Redcoats and the enslaved. Where

is Kate, owned by the Russells? Rose and Venus,
by the Cutlers? Underground radar might locate

bones the way it finds water and sewer pipes.
Black soldiers battled here—Ishmael, Cato, Cuff…

I open the hot mailbox to my gas bill, *Viking Travel,*
and the ACLU needing my vote. A fall leaf drops.

SPECIAL DELIVERY

from the archives of the US Postal Museum

Tell me, someone, is it time
for James to arrive by Parcel Post from a mile away,
a mere fifteen cents of a boy, eight months old,
sent by his parents to stay with his grandmother,
who waits on the porch under a rippling flag,
an infant dressed like it was Sunday morning church,
where sweat streaks his thick hair,
James, son of Jesse and Mathilda Beagle,
about to be dropped off in Batavia, Ohio in 1913,
insured for fifty dollars, according to postal reports,
tucked into the mail bag like a puppy,
too frightened to cry, stunned by housewives
petting his face and cooing, not knowing where
he's going or why, who the large man is
his parents trusted to carry him across ruts and stones—
Tell me, how is the boy holding up?
Baby James, as the newspapers called him,
seared into his pre-memory the rough canvas
scraping his legs, then hands lifting him
into flashing sun and something flapping at his face.

LOCAL DINER AT 5 PM

Dinner time for children and old folks, macaroni and cheese,
hot dogs and coleslaw,
though old is a definition up for grabs,
and children might be of any age—

Jerry's mother orders pot roast and mashed potatoes,
no vegetables, no salad,
I want to go home,
she says to the waiter.

You live in Florida, Jerry says, *you're staying with us for now.*

In the next booth, a couple with a toddler.
She smacks the table hard in front of the boy,
Eat your mashed potatoes now.

We glance over, then look away, it's not our business,
the woman's had it with something,
the man's saying nothing.
She smacks the table again.

Jerry's mother needs help cutting the roast beef
into small bites,
smooshing the butter and salt,
What is this? she asks.

I think I'm already dead, she tells the woman
whose toddler sobs.

I'll beat you when we get home,
the woman growls at the boy,
as the man pays the bill.

Do we say something? Will it make her hit him harder?
People are staring,
the waiter turns his back.

I never got hit as a child, did you? Jerry asks me.

My mother was a slapper, I say.
It was common.
I pick at my chicken pot pie,
stab wilted lettuce.

We're going to get your favorite chocolate ice cream now,
Jerry tells his mother,
as he signals the waiter.

The couple stand the toddler on the floor,
snot dripping into his mouth.
We should have said something, I say,
as the door closes behind them.

Jerry's mother doesn't seem to hear,
she's moving bits of meat into circles.
I want to go home,
she tells the meat.

THE FATHER OF WESTERN SURGERY IN TENTH CENTURY ANDALUSIA SPAIN

Dr. Al-Zahrawi paces his hospital ward,
weighing
whether to drill into the skull of young Hasan—

unlike his hostile pagan neighbors, he knows
evil spirits
don't exit through a bloody hole in the head—

but the frantic boy at the edge of puberty
can't sleep or eat;
his head throbs; he rages about a goatherd.

Al-Zahrawi knows this herder: he sutured
his shoulder
with cat gut, cauterized the gash above his eye.

It's said this surgeon loved his students
as his children,
so I've written into this poem his kindness

toward Hasan, raped on his noonday hillside hike
by the goatherd,
who bloodied him, stood over him, and laughed.

And I invented Hasan, whose story the doctor
asks to hear.
They walk into the citrus and olive tree garden,

slowly breathing the blossomed air, the drill
and notebook
stored. The doctor bends to whisper, *I believe you.*

AESOP'S CROWS

I can hear the phone ring all night in Dad's empty
bedroom. Stop the mail. Cancel *National Geographic.*

The zebras won't suffer. But the birds? Who's greasing
rainspouts so squirrels skid into the driveway and miss

the feeder? Robber baron crows must know—no more
BBs from Dad's porch window. Gutters ice-jammed.

A pile of yellowing undershirts on the basement floor.
Snow wafts off the firs in poofs like the milkweed

the Wampanoag used to stanch the blood
this land is built on. The part of the day I rued?

Twelve to three—no time to get to the hospital.
Long distance updates, Dad turning blue.

Crows are highly intelligent. Some can kill a toxic toad,
pluck its edible innards out by flipping it on its back.

Aesop thought them wise. In the "Crow and the Pitcher,"
the thirsty bird uses pebbles to make the water rise.

For years a talking crow visited us, voice in the trees
like a spirit from the underworld. A neighbor shot it dead.

SEEDING THE FLOWERBED

for my father

My scarf mustard, scalloped at my neck,
  my coat and hat wool, boots black—

having had my say with mourning, I step
  into morning's ampersand, a sonic wreck

of garbage trucks and recycled tin
  dogging my dog walk on feather-thin

snow streaked russet, down to the playground
  where we'd munched scones, and you, stung

on the ear, found the yellow jacket nest,
  tunneled deep beneath the grass fast

seeding the town flowerbed. Your swift foot
  filled the openings with mulch and dirt,

angry dive-bombers scoured the thwarted
  passageways, abuzz with what they courted,

but couldn't reach, while you swatted and shouted,
  mica-studded gravel of endings, besotted

with being, your afternoon with me on the bench,
  my sense it was your last, only a hunch.

IN THE COMPANY OF NIGHTMARE

Her father's lawyer friend asked what I knew.
Before I heard about her death, I knew.

What should I have told him? She was alone
while her husband slept? Her father knew

how scared she was, but stayed away? Waited
three days for a hospital bed to open, knowing

she was depressed, a therapist ashamed
to become a patient, savvy enough to know

a label survives in indelible ink? Her husband
took her dancing to cheer her up. She didn't say no,

because she couldn't, or why bother, or why not
let him pretend dancing could save her. Nothing

mattered at that point, just the rope flung
over a beam in the basement, the decision *Never,*

no matter what, to enter the hospital where
she had worked, where people would *know*.

After Katherine's birth, I lived with despair,
didn't sleep or eat. I paced the hallway, knowing

I was slipping into dangerous ideation, afraid
close friends would leave. She did, with no

apology, her mother's psychotic breaks a red
flare blinking in her mirror, my pain nothing

to hers, my healthy baby no one she welcomed.
Each miscarriage for her, a breach for us. I knew

her rage at me would sharpen. To use her name now
would be cruel. Did I return her last call? No.

RIVER BIRCH

Whose river fed my trees their name, swollen in spring
run-offs, deep in the country where old men putter on porches
with broken lamps and sealed tins of molasses bread?

Only love can break a heart, we used to sing, and this late
in our lives we know how the valve of compassion hardens,
what each friendship takes in the way of forgiveness.

It's easy to lose each other, the way a rockslide can start
with one rock, and the park where Scouts broke camp
becomes a ruin of shattered trees and buried trails.

Once I tried to get you back. I learned nothing, except
it's awful to bear the death of a tree, empty space
where branches protected me from a stranger's stare.

River of fine sediment building banks, wearing down rocks.
Today I see sooty scars in the bark—I will call
an arborist—but maybe I see brokenness everywhere.

THE MAN IN THE HAT

They used to be whole, but now they are parts.
His leg strewn across baggage claim, her hand severed on her lap.
The boy who once had eyes. Coal black and soft.
Over there a wheelchair covered in downed wires.
A bloody foot stuck on the footrest.
One scream does not sound like another.
Uniforms run back and forth at a loss,
wheel the bodies on luggage carts, on rolling suitcases
strung together like a train of toy wagons.
Somewhere history is gloating. It's still alive.
Somewhere a man in a light jacket and dark hat
may be watching the footage on TV, eating his dinner,
or strolling through another city making notes of targets.
Maybe he went home first to kiss his mother.
She loved him. She was a good mother, after all.

ISOTOPES

In Fukushima, wild boars from the mountains
    graze in abandoned yards and gardens,

eat radioactive crops without dying,
    rut by hedges, defecate on streets.

Tainted, they breed in empty houses, squat
    on tatami mats, males two hundred pounds.

People left years ago, dishes still in the sink
    at the restaurant where boar was a delicacy,

mounds of decayed vegetables in the grocery collapsing
    the shelves as rats ransack the sludge.

The poisoned dirt bagged and ready to go,
    but where? And how to get rid of the beasts?

Three mass graves in Nihonmatsu hold 1,800 boars,
    no public land left to use except maybe schools.

Hired hunters try to bury them, but dogs dig them up,
    and now who can trust the dogs, running like wolves.

In Soma, a new crematorium filters isotopes
    from smoke. It can only burn three boars a day.

Not enough people want to work stuffing body parts
    down the stacks, first cutting them to fit.

Cesium-137 has a half-life of thirty years.
    The government says to its people—

we'll make it safe, plant new fields, we can't pay
    to keep you in other towns.

The government says, *Come home.*

THE CYCLE

A voice rose from the rhododendron
outside my window where grackles sleep.

You must stop thinking so much.

Catfish sailed on silver threads above my head.
Alarm rang the alarm.

I snoozed. A catfish caught by a cat sizzled up
in a fry pan loaded with salt. I snoozed again.

I was the cat who hunted the catfish, lugged
it home in my jaws so I could eat it.

I was the catfish in the cat's teeth, bumped along
then dumped on the ground, praying eyes open.

The chef? That was me, too: chopping off
the catfish head, happy with my slaughter.

PYTHAGORAS SAID THE SOUL OF HOMER MOVED INTO A PEACOCK

My peacock is strutting on the deck again.
I thought it was in ancient Samos, but no,

its hundred eyes track me in the kitchen,
as I knead my floured mound of dough,

listen to NPR—the bees are dying off,
maybe the yellow jackets. They've lived

in the cracks of the brick patio for years
and stung my thighs through white cotton.

Maybe, like the peacock, they're immortal,
their silence a kind of holiness.

When my cousin Danuta's husband had a stroke,
she used her eyes and voice for his.

Believe me, I am not good at praying for people.
My mind wanders. I see peacock feathers catch

glints of sun from the window, and Homer's
soul opens like a peony in the garden.

It's said the Dalai Lama brings a peacock feather
to his audiences with the holy and the desperate.

I've learned my Polish grandmother kept a peacock
as a security system. It shrieked when the Nazis

stormed her road, but she and my young aunt and uncle
had fled weeks earlier on the last ship for New York.

Before my grandfather died, he called for his prized
canaries, decades gone, trained by his Victrola.

In the hospital they sang for him all night.

LUNAR ECLIPSE, WATERVILLE VALLEY

At the cusp of the road winding into a field of stars,
I focus my small binoculars.

Wind whips the back of my neck, hisses
at my need to find you out here,

where no one can find *me*.

I hope the crimson shadow will look
like the cut I planted in your cheek

with my pencil when you chased me
up the basement stairs, enraged,

the coal furnace behind us like a red dragon—

or the jagged bite in your left hand
when you saved me from a cornered racoon.

I trip on ice mounds, welcome deer tracks,
coyote howls, the scat of squirrels—

all signs of you waiting for me.

~

I'm here to confess: I didn't get to you in time,
a magpie grabbed my voice on the phone.

A wolf pinned me to my kitchen floor,
two white leopards blocked the doors.

And the ghost of Mom sang an eerie song
about Emma crying all night if I left town.

Your nurse said, *He's 95, he'll stay*
on oxygen forever.

Dad, I know it happened fast:
the oxygen mask you refused:

Take it off. I won't live like this.
I hear you took it off yourself.

Bring that animal spirit to me now,
while I'm still open to it,

before some numbskull tells me
I should go inside, or I'll freeze.

II Poland: A Fugue

SHORTWAVE RADIO: SEPTEMBER 1, 1939

Was it in the White Mountains, near Mt. Jefferson, by the Mad River in
Thornton,

under a tarp in rain, under stars, a gibbous moon, by firelight, by flashlight,

could they afford sleeping bags, or did wool blankets girdle them against

the ground grown cold in late summer's turning, were they listening for
nothing

in particular, or piecing together warnings, did they hear it in passing as
the radio

signals ebbed or were the voices strong, almost as if the cities of the earth

bullhorned their cry in a pocket of forest, did they drop their flasks and beer
bottles

or catch a shoe in the fire, and how many men were with my father, Polish
immigrants

counting hours off from their jobs, the fish they'd caught and fried and salted

and the ones they'd thrown back for next time, how long did the broadcast last,

telling them what they knew without being told—*Your family will eat dust
behind tanks,*

your village will be fire without water, and you who got out can do nothing.

THAT ALLEY OF OUR CHILDHOOD

An alley made into a garden made an escape for us
when the adults talked politics, thrashed newspapers,
the words *Nazi* and *Russian* like salt and pepper on steak
sandwiches we took outside in waxed paper, stripping
crust for the sparrows scouring the asphalt, lighting
on the white peony that threatened to topple
like the lost world they were in there ranting about,
this small garden of respite planted to perfection
where we didn't know the names of flowers and no one
could tell us in English, but we knew what the body
knows, that the sun makes happiness in our skin
and the velvet yellow rose with the tangerine stripe
crushed to our nose makes our head float and soar
to the kingdom we built with stones and worms,
dirt, and a garden hose long enough to circle
like a river and protect like a moat the noble house
we fashioned which nothing could crush, not even war.

IT HAPPENED ALL THE TIME

Buczkowice, Poland, 1912

Daylight shatters through the thatches where a bird might fall,
two days since she boiled eggs, baked black bread, scrubbed potatoes,

the orbit of hands and feet circumferential to her mind's rutted track,
drawn curtain, its window onto wind-ravaged fields where hay withers,

one breath at a time, questions circle like wolves down from the north
to haunt the tattered sheep's pen, barn stalls overflowing with udders

untouched since morning. Not old enough to talk, the child, his snagged
breath in the blankets like wool in the coats his father weaves

in the factory up the road by the bend in the river. Or should I say
my grandfather weaves—the child, my uncle no one ever mentioned,

because *It happened all the time*. Who could grieve over an empty cradle
when it would fill soon? Maybe with a boy to weave the cloth,

patch the roof, ward off Kommandants and Soviet troops, unlike the one
who might not have lived through it all anyway.

THE NINE CHILDREN OF MARIANNA GLUZA

who died   before the age of eighteen   torment my father
who is dead   he didn't   mention   them
his first cousins   what does it mean   if your family
erases you   as a child   was the grief   of your death
too much   to bear   or were you   replaceable
another bulb in the garden   another   late-night mattress
soaked with longing   or duty   another rosary
I confess   it is not just my father   tormented

*trauma takes the tong*ue   historians of trauma write
smothers the cradle   but facts don't die
so easily   I found his mountain village   House 186
where he lived   with my grandmother   during WWI
his aunt Marianna   her children   three died there
Marianna   I said   *Marianna*   as I walked   the house
starvation   or typhus   cholera   the Flu
Natalia   aged 4   yelled *Tadek*   my father   didn't answer
he was watching   the family peacock   Maria   aged 3
coughing in bed   so much phlegm   I choked
my father   ran out   into the snowstorm

two   children   wailed   until   they didn't
I saw   my grandmother Teresa   in Philadelphia
white apron   aunt   of eight   dead nieces and nephews
no   I forgot one

in that house   a child's sled   a painted chair
a bullet hole   in the wall   an abandoned   bird's nest
the frame   and sinews   of a family   knit
together   my cousins   met me   in the village
grandchildren   of Marianna's   three daughters
who survived   but they only   knew so much
there was the Second War   forced labor
the camps   and

this I know   my father   boycotted funerals
when he couldn't comfort   the bereaved
didn't visit me   in the hospital   at eighteen
in college   alone   four hours away   by car
a blood clot   in my leg   swollen twice its size
said he was certain   I'd be okay
was terrified   of death   I tell myself now

my cousins   Teresa and Zbyzisk   on All Souls'
lit candles   with me   on family graves   at dusk
we found Marianna   with her husband   among
the rows of tombstones   bouquets   lanterns
vines   across   her barely   legible   name

Buczkowice, Poland, 2017

MY COUSIN ZBYSZEK VISITS HIS DEAD AUNT WALERIA ON ALL SOULS' DAY

Bielsko, Poland, 2017

when does   the wind   not blow   here
as if   the starved   tortured   shot in camps
in streets   in beds   want   us   to know
we live   an illusion   of   safety
our candlelight dinners   down-filled duvets
children prancing   in spring   like ponies

we circle   the cemetery's   monuments
wind down   lanes   where families   cart
bags of apples   flowers   small glass jars
at Waleria's   grave   Zbyszek   wipes
dust   from her name   *I want   you   to know*
your brother   Uncle Tadeusz   didn't die
in Germany   he escaped   to America
after   he heard   his parents   siblings
were executed   by   Russian   squads
he died   not knowing   it wasn't   true
I just   told   my mother   she wept

Zbyszek pauses as if waiting for Waleria
to understand the wind flaps paper bags
he hands me an apple lights a candle
it matters just to exist I hear her answer
Waleria young woman missing
twelve years four in German camps
eight in the Gulag as suspected
troublemaker anti-Nazi presumed dead
Christmas Eve 1952 Waleria returns
husband two children their eyes dim stars
in a black sky I start to say *how awful*

be happy Zbyszek scolds me frowning
the past is the past who am I to say *no*
naïve American I want to know how
this history lives in me lived in my father
I tell him that is why I listen to the dead

Zybszek   lays   a spray   of white mums
on Waleria's   grave   kneels   on one knee
families   stream past   pushing   strollers
a young woman   green eyes   like balsam
high-heeled black boots   yellow scarf
places   a white candle   red lantern
on the grave   says a prayer   near Zbyszek
who startles   at   this stranger   touching
his arm   *Waleria   was   my grandmother*

FORCED LABOR

for Halina Cader

Thrust into the *platz,* wobbly-legged, bleating what boys bleat
when they're on the bench, sized up and down, how strong,

how much will he eat, can he learn German, and his momma,
will beatings knock her out of him, does he have lice, a disease

we can catch, will he outgrow his bed, need to bathe in the house,
will he escape, get a message to Krakow, scare off the Scouts.

What would he be good at—the plow, the tractor, the mower—
Could he learn to prune, harvest apples, keep bees, chop wood,

and what should we do with him later, after years of this slave boy
in his shack by the barn, a young man, keen on sexual things

young men get killed for when it isn't their right, can never be,
their blood *subhuman,* brains primitive, by then old enough

to anger our village wanting to see the lot of them dead, not
a bedraggled ghost snatched from a market in Poland,

his life wrung from him like wine from a flattened flask.

TWO POTATOES AND A DOG, 1939

Buczkowice, Poland

Because Szymon couldn't find his mother
he cut all the fur off the dog.
It looked like a spotted pig.
In the kitchen by the cold stove,
he cradled and swaddled it,
he made it need him,
the dog who waited by the door at night
and barked if a rifle rustled a branch
on the dirt road to the house.
That was the day his father's train departed,
the afternoon he found his father's note—
They are coming for me, they're here—
while his mother stood in the neighbor's field
where she'd hidden two potatoes for dinner,
crying, it must have been, to the Black Madonna
whose mutilated face shone through sheaves of wheat,
the scars bleeding again with the words,
I don't believe I will see you again.
And when his mother came home
carrying two potatoes, she said nothing.
She looked at the dog and said nothing.

THE SECOND TIME

for my cousin Jan Gluza

You dragged your right foot, round as a melon, clawed
an ash tree, fell, then hauled your swollen body
back to the dirt road, drooled and spat and coughed
so hard you could be heard in farmhouses by the river—

you were EH-23662, leftist troublemaker—
after 56 days of reeducation and torture in Auschwitz, freed.

A hilltop shimmered in your delirium, a Galician sturgeon
parted your hair with its fin, your love bathed in your eyes until
she rose from the tub like an alabaster figurine on the sea,
the workers' tract you'd printed sprouted blue wings.

Some star must have led you home, some burgeoning path
of cow dung, or notes left by friends:
one kilometer, find water and bread in box behind fence.

Bloated like a seal, weak as a milkweed stalk, feverish,
cossetted by family, medicated, urged to escape—

you would have none of it, you went back to your press,
and the Gestapo came for you, all spit-polished and sure.

TO THE YOUNG PROTESTANTS HOLDING PORTRAITS OF MARTIN LUTHER ON THE STEPS OF THE CATHOLIC CEMETERY IN BIELSKO ON ALL SOULS' DAY

When Luther couldn't convert his Jewish neighbors, he wrote:

Set fire to their synagogues and schools in honor of our Lord
and of Christendom, that God might see we are Christians.

Between us iron grates and the cries of blackbirds on graves.
Wind circles the firs. A child bounces a red ball.

You stand smiling after five hundred years. You ask for nothing
more than a coin from history, the blessing of pigeons nibbling

crumbs at your feet, but it was never this simple. How young
I was when my parents converted from Catholicism, entered

the plain nave of a Protestant chapel and its Bach cantatas.
Condemned by priests, shunned by our Irish relatives,

we became devout Presbyterians. My Polish grandfather,
a religious and political rebel, wouldn't let a priest in his house.

In Sunday school, I was taught about the Reformation's doctrines,
martyrs, exiles. What can a child understand of cruelty

and dogma? I missed my cousins in their First Communion
finery, their frosted cakes. In Europe, in Ireland, death came

for centuries with the swing of a censer, a bare cross replacing
the crucifix, families divided with the slice of a cake knife.

We stand in this land where *the people of the book* visit us
in the fall wind—Jews and Christians, who've strayed,

says the Quran, from God's true faith. *Enough,* the blackbirds cry.

BRUNO SCHULZ FROM THE BARDO

with words by Amos Oz

Heat, filthy, gut-sick heat in my city's cobblestone streets.

I hear Bennu aims to split a continent or two. What kind of God does
    that?

It looks like a saltwater wedge has surged into the dry Mississippi, could
    poison tap water.

Amos Oz—the kind of man I could have been, a run on sentence asserting
    itself.

Elon Musk, beaten by his father for being beaten by his friends, loves
    Mars.

A baguette, how absurd that I died carrying oblong bread, fragrant with
    yeast.

My Nazi owner fought with his friend; each shot the other's "personal
    Jew."

I died in the streets many times before and after that.

What political cant does for the lonely: the mob's chant warms your ear.

Oz wanted to grow up to be a book, not a writer. If I had been a book...

It's frankly tiresome to watch my life story repeat—and unoriginal.

On Mars, assuming there aren't already Martians, will my dying finally
    end?

How brilliant—plans to outwit Bennu while we let the glaciers melt.

Beginning to tell a story is like making a pass at a total stranger at a restaurant.

My short stories are more like poems, some say. *A poem is like a one-night stand.*

I see my Polish city's now in Ukraine, invaded by the latest hordes.

Elon, I have no faith in Mars. Maybe in a book, not the author.

That mural I painted on the Nazi's wall? An ocean voyage set in a desert.

LINES BY WISŁAWA SZYMBORSKA REARRANGED AS ELEGY

All imperfection is easier to tolerate in small doses.
I'm working on the world, revised, improved edition.
Those crafty hedgehogs drafting aphorisms after dark.

The exam is History of Mankind.
Two monkeys, chained to the floor, sit on the windowsill.
Don't ask, I can't say, I don't know.

To tell right from wrong, "ours" from "theirs."
You'll see how we give birth among the ruins.
A rose? A rose? What could that be?

The most pressing questions are naive ones.
All the cameras have gone to another war.
History rounds off skeletons to zero.

Forgive me, distant wars, for bringing flowers home.
In my dreams I paint like Vermeer van Delft.
A little poem, a sigh, at the cost of indescribable losses.

TONGUE OF THE EARTH

Pablo Neruda sits on my couch, watching tree shadows spiral
on my blue wall. He's reading Szymborska. Poor dog, he says,
staring at my old terrier on the floor: he can't see, he can't hear,
he can't even read Szymborska. Hurricane winds are coming.
A little poem, a sigh, at the cost of indescribable losses, he reads
out loud, and the dog rouses to the rhythm of shoes on the floor,
opens his jaws to catch the music on his tongue. Music, mother
tongue of the earth. Asked at a dinner what books he loved,
my father said, *How to Speak Dog* and *View with a Grain of Sand,*
and everyone laughed about the dog. I miss my father, I tell Pablo,
and he looks at me with large sad eyes. *Forgive me, distant wars,*
for bringing flowers home, Szymborska wrote in her message
to the world. The winds are picking up.

IMMIGRANT MOBILE

Peabody Essex Museum, Alexander Calder Exhibit

What to call it?

Mobile,

Duchamp told Calder.

Something that moves,

and also French for motive.

I wish I'd thought of that, thought Einstein

in 1943,

at the Museum of Modern Art,

watching Calder's *A Universe*

spin its ninety cycles

in forty minutes.

~

If my father were alive,

I'd sit him down over herring in white wine

and a nip of cognac.

He'd hear about the two summers

I walked the winding lanes

of Buczkowice,

until I found the mountain chalet

where he was born in 1913

two days after his father sailed for America.

He'd learn the names of cousins I visit every year,

descendants of the family

he never revealed.

We'd talk this time about what happened in the First War—

~

How mobile can an immigrant be,

floating

among houses and continents

like *metal made weightless,*

arcing through space on a breath or a breeze?

~

What happened in that chalet, who was left?

His aunt lost nine children.

Behind

Calder's metal plates,

shadows swirl on the walls

in their own dark mobiles.

~

I study a plaque:

A mobile leaves

an invisible wake behind it.

~

Shoeless children begged in the streets.

The colors of hunger, the village historian

called the red, green, and purple soups

made from tree roots.

~

Ten years old when he met his father,

separated by war,

then by America, hostile

to Jews, Hungarians, Poles, Southern Italians,

just before the quotas.

~

The mobiles, bright red and black and white,

orderly and signifying no content

but movement, gravity, wind.

The shadows in spotlight

distort, merge, and break apart.

~

What did this war stir in him?

An orbit of silence. Spells of despair.

A daughter afraid to ask.

~

And what of the *immobile*,

left behind in the wake

of a ship leaving port?

STEFANIA TAKES THE ELLIS ISLAND LITERACY TEST, READING BIBLE PASSAGES IN HER NATIVE LANGUAGE

I must read louder for this translator
I am weary with my groaning;
In my bowels, in my ribs, in my temple bone
All the night make I my bed
On his ruined shirt, on his shrunken chest, on his collar bone
To swim;
I shifted when the ship shifted, I turned when he vomited,
I wept when I saw the Statue in the harbor
I water my couch
My suitcase is my couch, my chair, my table
I water my couch with my tears;
But I must not cry in front of them
Who is a wise man and endued with knowledge among you?
Our men know hunger
Let him shew out of a good conversation
But I can say only hello, goodbye,
Yes, no, in English, my husband
Mumbles hello, it sounds like hell
I must read louder for this translator
Let him shew out of a good conversation
His works with meekness of wisdom
Why not strength of wisdom?
My eye is consumed because of grief
But my eye must not be red,
Must see every word
The getting of treasures by a lying tongue
A false witness shall perish
My husband's job is on paper only
If his cousins find out I'm pregnant
They will throw us out

THE EYES OF OUR PAST

To turn an eyelid inside out,
a button hook beats a hair pin.
It hooks the lid, holds it up,
then flips the folded rim.

The spider veins, the socket
bones and filaments, the iris
a brown or green or blue nugget
in a scrim of fluid—

the eye waters, the light burns,
of course, the eye wants to blink,
shrink back from the hook,
even the closed eye turns—

But the Button-Hook Men
see fast, see deep in swollen
pockets: trachoma, white omen
of deportation from Ellis Island.

Wailing children, women, men
clutch one-way tickets back.
The Button-Hook Men move on
where lines of eyelids wait.

WHEN SYRINX TURNS INTO A LILAC BUSH

On the hill of lilacs at the Arboretum, blue blossoms peak
on hardy stems, as if Syrinx, safe from Pan, reveled

in noonday sun, and Whitman, tired of mourning,
clipped a branch, not for a coffin but the vase on his desk.

I planted three lilac trees in the rock garden my father built,
the blue my favorite, lasting long after the others died,

a miracle of sorts, since I was a negligent gardener,
harming the trees I loved but didn't know how to save.

Some say Pan chased Syrinx because he loved her beauty;
others say he tried to rape her; maybe it was both.

My daughter and I vacationed at the Wentworth Hotel,
named for the Tory governor who left behind a lilac garden,

the first in America, copied by Washington and Jefferson,
the Persian *lilak* seeding itself into American history.

At fifteen I found *Leaves of Grass* in my father's bookcase:
Whitman's narcissistic self-love, obsessive sex, shocked me.

Chosen to seek foreign and unweathered shores, I wrote about
myself that night in my first poem. Many years later I'd find

in my father's mountain village the family he'd never named,
survivors of the Hapsburgs, Hitler, then Stalin,

and two centuries hell-bent on erasing their language—
upended by immigration to America—our *wretched refuse.*

My daughters have become what I call full Americans, free
from the weight of otherness and migration stories,

my father's and grandparents' papers pressed under books
in trunks, irrelevant, unless found by a curious child.

III

ODE TO TEASED HAIR

I spend a lot of money to look this cheap, Dolly Parton twanged
in her white suede miniskirt and fringed jacket, her lips
a gobsmacking vermillion, her wig teased like a halo in San Marco.

When Covid bodies piled up in freezer trucks for months,
two mourning doves swoosh-landed on my windowsill daily,
feathers puffed up all bouffant, beaks locked, half-cocked in lust—

A memory of myself with a teased mop in high school shot up until
I shot it down like a drone. Boys wore leather in our blue-collar zone,
girls teased. Kids across the highway went to college and France.

Then again, Dolly Parton, born in a one-room cabin on the banks
of Little Pigeon River, whupped her *dirt poor* life into shape by singing
about dirt poor *luck*—but she couldn't be smart if she couldn't talk right.

Through quarantine I studied Giacometti, O'Keefe, Cezanne, Basquiat.
One day glancing up from *Dustheads,* I saw the male dove flutter
onto the female, almost fall off, but hang on for five seconds.

To shame a people, just call them dumb. Mock their accent,
their English. Dolly learned business from her illiterate daddy.
As a child, I wanted Christmas doves to lift me out of the zone.

Dolly sends millions of books to poor kids, calls it *Imagination Library.*
Don't teach them their letters, the masters taught, or you'll be sorry.
My daddy loved books: *They take you where you can't go.*

BIRD'S NEST WITH RIBBON

I thrive in late autumn, when my yard shuns color for musty brown,
buttons down its reckless blossoming, and the city folds up

its red patio umbrellas. Summer is a daytime nightmare—
beach goers in flip flops, kids with tennis rackets, women in white—

far from the asphalt heat on blue-collar stoops, haze of factory smoke
that left me morose as a child, waiting for evening's first breeze.

A day with high humidity, high heat, plunges me into isolation.
I want to protect my body from the memory of heat.

If I go out on days like that, I see the man who pushes his wealth
in a grocery cart, black garbage bags shining in harsh sunlight,

his water bottle strapped to the handle—I don't always say hello.
Just now, I noticed yellow leaves fluttering from a river birch,

the last few, and a nest in the bare branches outside my study window.
A blue-and-white-striped parade ribbon dangles from the twigs.

HAPPY HOUR WITH CHAUCER

Geoffrey, this might sound ludicrous, but
I miss you.
Please come sip brandy on my balcony.

I can see you, sly and full of gossip, keen-
eared, bearded,
naming the birds in my English plane tree,

delighted by the two mourning doves
who mate
on my railing each April, puffed up and clumsy.

You might like my neighbors—horny trekkers,
the pot-bellied,
swaggering lech and the sagging centerfold.

Who you are as a writer isn't the same as—
what?
Your bootlicking snobbery, corrupt business...

All those weekends I spent with you,
my friend—
college days in a stiff neck brace, alone,

sounding out your hammered pentameter until
you spoke
to me and I woke up thinking in Middle English.

We can bear what we think unbearable, Seneca thought.
And you,
banished from your Customs House post, home,

and social circle, turned to your imaginary pilgrims,
as did I,
their squabbling voices, raucous jokes a distraction

from my doctor's prognosis that I might never really
walk again.
I could read, so I could travel beyond my body.

I learned how to divert my mind like a tributary
passing
through granite, like a Stoic—not to feel, but to think

my way through fear, memorizing your stanzas
at night
when music from the quad shook my room.

In time, the doctor proved a quack. But trauma lies
in cells,
startles awake with a nightmare or a crack of light.

I think I learned how to rout my awfulizing mind
through you.
Visit me, listen to The Centerfold thump The Lech.

GIFTS OF STONE

The lapis lazuli pendant you gave me,
with bits of gold flickering
in midnight blue like stars over Mt. Sinai,

hangs from a sterling silver chain
above my breastbone.
When sun heats the metal, I hear the strum

of a honeybee dive-bombing yellow peonies
in the rock garden—
the honeybee of our marriage, mad for nectar,

seeding mellow seasons and yellow fruitfulness
in our years of amazed
husbandry, two daughters born after a fallow time.

Inanna wears royal blue lapis into the underworld.
Afghan miners on mules
scale mountains at daybreak to find it.

Cleopatra brushes her lids with the blue powder.
Botticelli grinds stones
to make ultramarine for Mary's cape.

The lapis bird of prey you brought me
from Chile, a gift I disliked,
peers at me from a bookshelf while I work.

Nonsense, you insisted, it's a parrot.
Still, its amber eye unnerves,
shifting in a shifting light, and squints,

the bird rustling in my ear: "No, not *that* word.
Hunt for the right one
with the full throttle of a bee in an open bud."

PAEAN

Out of our bodies we made a world, named
after ourselves, not knowing
whether it harbored a rage we might never understand,
or a god come to save us.
We held what we made, trembling,
the bassinet wheeled in and out,
mouse-like squeals of tiny lungs in warm air,
always the milk of inadequacy in our mouths
as though the question *What do we do now?*
wasn't ancient, not the mother tongue
that ushers us to the door where someone
hushes the donkey, builds a fire,
then kneels down on parched earth to pray.

~

When I woke in sweat, saying I didn't want to die,
you licked my tears
until my skin grew smooth as cheeks
washed with brown sugar and water;
but I did want to die, too, I didn't want to be
alone with my fear, to bow down before my broken body.
You bought none of that. I cradled next to you
in fistfuls of dreaming, where a fox came to my roost
and paced. How cold the morning light,
breaking in with its bossiness: you hadn't slept,
I could see, you had purple shadows for eyes.
When you rose to walk the dog, snow fell
on our bed, and it was beautiful and lethal
as Mt. Everest, the cliffs radiant with climbers.

~

You stood beside me on the hill, the waiting
over, thuds ricocheting into the valley, where farmers
woke to biscuits and eggs, the icy edge
of the path to the barn. We looked up to the cemetery
where your dead lay wreathed with Christmas greens.
Already they were making room next to your father—
the diggers in their dark hats with white fleece,
hauling dirt from the freezing ground,
carving a deep hole for her small urn.
Your hand gripped mine, mourning buttoned like a coat,
its tie too tight, its cuffs shiny and worn,
in its pocket your mother's single refrain—
Where am I? I want to go home—and there was no home
but this place, chosen long ago for its view.

~

You carried me across ravines when flood waters
rose above your knees, you pulled me from the forest
as lightning felled the trees and every songbird died,
but the death of thunder didn't dissolve my grief.
I'd become deaf to the timbre of the brook,
the crickets in our window boxes,
even the tenderness of your knock on my door.
Let me lead you now across that field
of buttercups, loosestrife's riot of purple,
across a doorsill that opens into our sanctuary,
to windows scraped clean from winter.
I have dismantled the altar draped
with black cloth, the handprints
of regret. We carry ourselves.

SOMETIMES, THE MOON

This morning branches brush against the glass,
sixty small panes with concave centers,
where light pools and refracts, but no one
outside can see into the front hall, or into
the living room where my white dog sleeps
on my off-white couch. This could be a tableau
from eighteenth century Avignon, poised
for a painter to add a bowl of red tulips
to the table where coffee steams in a cup.
Oh, the freedom and exhaustion of inventing
what I need each day before the sun arrives
at my desk late afternoon, turning the gold
picture frames of those I love—and those
I was supposed to love—into planes
flickering and cross-hatched on my wall:
times I allowed myself to dream or mourn!
Love, remember the night we got lost skiing
on Mt. Greylock, the moon hovering
with light and admonition? *This is the way*
you can lose your life, not paying attention
to where you entered, or when you turned.
The moon visits us when we're weary
or bedraggled and couldn't care less,
but some nights it watches when we're wrung
out from loving each other, keeping the dog
at our feet before we court the dead of sleep.

GHAZAL OF THE GOATS

Not the lyric song of shepherds, my love
bleats ungodly tunes in private. My unlovely

Irish tongue, Polish doom, a marriage made
for goats to butt heads by day, by night, love.

Goat Man Ches McCartney wed a Spanish
knife-thrower, his near-miss lethal lover.

In my act, you don't flinch, duck, scrape, or bow.
It appears you're an idiot for love.

Ches took to the road with a herd of goats,
a two-legged one who hopped—now *that's* love.

Dressed in goat skins, Crusoe and the Good Book
in tow, he preached smelly riffs on God's love.

I preach, too, you say: once would be enough.
Finnegan wakes in my blood. My love,

Thor's chariot was pulled by two Norse goats
he ate each night. He saved the bones, by love

restored them whole each day. As I do you.
Teresa means harvest, my love.

METAPHYSICS OF THE SEAHORSE

In a seagrass meadow, a male seahorse
gives birth, lunging like the yellow horse

on springs at the Vineyard's penny arcade
my daughter loved, the barrel-bellied horse

grinning, Emma thought, as if it remembered
her each year. A camera films the seahorse

expelling hundreds of *fry* in a murky froth
from his brood pouch. *Most seahorses*

don't survive—they're weak swimmers—
but Poseidon's chariot was pulled by seahorses.

Imagine the shock of Dr. Julius Caesar Aranzi
in 1587, cutting into a brain and finding seahorse-

shaped tissue in the temporal lobe, branding it
the *hippocampus,* sea monster horse,

not knowing it held the key to memory
and memory's loss. The mindful seahorse

can look forward and back at the same time
while staying put. *Me?* I'm a crab, not a seahorse.

THE APPLE DOES NOT FALL FAR FROM THE TREE

reads the yellow wooden plate hanging in my kitchen,
a Red Delicious with pert stem and waxed sheen,
nothing like the pocked apples we picked

in your childhood, climbing ladders into gnarled branches
on sun-spackled afternoons, cloth baskets burgeoning
like the market sacks we toted last year in Florence,

weighed down, exhilarated by the Fra Angelico frescoes
in San Marco. We scoured the stalls for prosciutto
and mozzarella on ciabatta, fresh figs, and tomatoes,

tucked apples in our purses for afternoon snacks.
We ruminated on the monks' cells with white walls,
Scenes from the Life of Christ in each,

flooded with light like the salt and pepper flocks
of pigeons descending on our bench in the piazza.
They pecked crumbs in the gravel, ganged up

on the poor gimpy one who couldn't get away—What draws them
to attack when snippets of bread and biscotti
marble the gravel like confetti at a chapel?

What drove the monks to their solitary life of prayer
and made us linger by *The Mocking of Christ*,
his eyes blindfolded, someone spitting at his head?

SAN PASQUAL

The flatware scuttle, snap of bottle tops—
I'm washing up. One hell
of a mess in the crock pot.

Kiro skulks, on the lookout for squirrels
that leap past the windows like acrobats.
I was meant to see something here.

Beats me what it is. The cactus jeweled
in a red pincushion flower, white tips
like pearls? Not that.

Don't worry. I'm not doing the list.
The hand-carved blue-eyed zebra from Santa Fe
is my reality check—

This isn't a poem about loneliness.
I lack nothing that I can see.
Not even a wooden statue of San Pasqual,

smiling Patron Saint of the Kitchen.
He hated to cook, one source says,
but was made chef in the monastery.

Another says he loved to cook
and watches over kitchens in New Mexico
to keep the tortillas soft.

The right attitude toward misery
can make people worship you.
Also, the right attitude toward bliss.

What good is his smile? I burned
the rutabaga and dry-docked
the fish in a poaching pan.

Why haunt yourself with someone
else's life? Why take a thing with wings
and make it the bird of sacrifice or rapture?

The flask on his belt, the donkey by his side,
some damp hollow in the arroyo
where they're resting before the trek back—

It's not nothing, after all. But close.

THE SEASON OF OUR SUNDERING

Under locust trees, in the blossoming park by Town Hall,
masked and unmasked walkers dip hands in the fountain pool,

cool on this hot day, a limbic throwback to summers
at Walden or Long Pond, a day's release from work.

Near a young pear tree, I sit on a stone bench in noon sun,
watch my country divide. *She that was great among the nations,*

Jeremiah grieved, *and princess among the provinces, how is she*
become tributary! She weepeth sore in the night. Our local ER doc

posts to the town Facebook list: *help us save lives, help us*
flatten the curve. Jeremiah was thrown into a cistern of mud,

despised. And whatever prayer is, I pray for the mocked
and the deniers. My breathlessness is easing. I can walk up stairs,

stroll here like the others. I have no God to talk to, though I try.

CAPPUCCINO QUARANTINE

purple primrose on the glass coffee table in late September light

the ache of you the pinched nerve of you the radiating heat

why and when stalled tongue blistered lips the gasp of wanting you

home in time to hear what can be said now how hard how lockdown

how long to wait the borders so guarded the guards so exhausted

what time says to time and first last words the need to make it right

the steam gone like you milk frothed dark roast on a dark day

NOONTIME

At noon the church bells roll a hymn across our roofs.
"Misses the B flat minor," my neighbor complains,

although I can't hear the notes she hears. I cried
in my childhood pew when I heard that hymn.

I know she's in her studio inking monoprints.
My husband walks the dog, I close my notebook for the day.

What were those tears for, *who* for? I'd discovered God
plays favorites, like teachers and coaches, like parents.

Oh, Lord, my God, the hymn tolls to shoppers at Whole Foods
across the street, as they strip the shelves of paper goods,

when I in awesome wonder... My neighbor prints her latest
image of the church tower as scaffolding without bricks.

She's afraid to leave her house—low immunity, bad lungs.
She says printmaking "keeps the wolves away."

Were my tears a clue to who I am now? Wary.
Vigilant. A blackbird. Last night I snapped the sun

as it set behind the steeple: gold light on the bronze bell.
A wing appeared in the picture but not the whole bird.

CUPID PERUSES *THE TIMES*

A curly-headed cupid, reading
on my balcony, rain-drenched
and naked, hand on chubby chin,
thinking, no doubt, about what
certain words mean—*delirious:*
the way his perfumed head feels?
Or *rapacious*: his appetite for gold-
tipped anything and honey skin?
And *resuscitate*—to raise up again
in Latin, the way Lazarus, risen
from his tomb in Bethany,
ate supper with his sister Martha.
As in: restored to daily walks
and the scent of lemon trees.
My cupid reads *ventilator,* thinks
Ventus, the night wind his mother—
wild black hair rising—
calls *the breath of the gods.*

ELEGY IN PRAISE OF AN ENDING

To shake the shadow of you, the weight of you, the gloomy
voice of you, dead and still torturing my morning tea,

I walk to Windsong, orchard that bears no fruit, a half-
mile above the Mad River, where we fished for trout.

A stone pillar pokes from the snow, ice capped. Terminus,
the Roman god of property markers and limits, frowns

at me from a low-flung cloud. What gift can I give him—
a blue jay feather, dog treat, crusty cookie—so he'll come

closer? He drops onto the pillar, hops off with a dancer's grace.
Boundaries, he says, staring at my swollen eyes, *and I don't*

mean land. I must be hallucinating.
Feather in hand, he whooshes upward to a frozen branch

for an aerial view. Sun smarts my eyes, the wind burrows
into my ears through my wool hat, my hands and feet sting.

Frostnip first, then frostbite, I know, but I want Terminus
to say more. *Don't let anyone cross the line,* he intones

like an augur at the palace, *even the dead.* He means you.
I couldn't hold your pain without losing myself. Then, now.

A vision of you shimmers on the snow: clawing at my coat,
furious. The nutty deity lifts a finger. My kick sends you flying.

POSTSCRIPT

You’re wasting time. Your lilac needs pruning. By the shed,
split birch rots, the compost is amuck in rainwater.

Remember your lemon summers, a table set by a stone wall, peaches
in a basket with white napkins. Tart apples and Stilton on plates.

You've forgotten how to laugh. Tongue in ear. Toes on thigh.
Where did you put your body, once taut with expectation?

Who could know what would happen. Ice storms out of season.
Winter moth in the trees. Spores rising in blades of grass.

Others picked apple blossoms and put them in a blue vase,
while you filled hand-made journals with complaint.

The stones are tired of hearing your story. *Bitter, bitter* the crows
pronounce mid-flight. You should hike down to the pond

late afternoon now that your legs will carry you. Go ahead:
take your clothes off: your broken body is not special.

Feel the silt slide across hair rising like milkweed.
Feet sinking in mossy sludge, you'll kick off from the bottom

as it dissolves beneath you.

URBAN RIVER RUN

"Who hears the fishes when they cry?"

Thoreau asked,
after paddling the Concord and Merrimack
for two weeks with his brother John,

years before his cabin and beans,
before he accidentally
set the woods on fire.

He woke to sunrise on the water rippling
his canoe in light soft as a ripe peach,

pushed off into cold water rinsing him of Concord's orderly
prosperity,

nothing but the lure of what he didn't know ahead of him,
what he would see that would change him—

~

Immigrants from the Pilgrims onward
lived on river herring, shad, salmon.
Silver running they'd called
the spring herring migrations so abundant
they colored the rivers,

fish swarming inland from the Atlantic,

back to their home rivers to spawn,
then back to the sea.

Instead, Henry saw few of the fish of his childhood,
their paths trapped behind dams,

thinned out and ghostly—
an ancient food chain vanishing beneath his paddle.

~

Henry and John called for the good men of Sudbury,
Wayland, and Concord to take a crowbar to the Billerica dam.
Then Henry went to the woods to write about river fish.

~

At the Mystic Dam, my husband and I stand
on metal grates,
looking down into a fish ladder,

portal for Alewife river herring trying to reach
the upper lake where seagulls loop and dive.

A woman plays guitar and sings, a man and boy kneel
to count herring
with us, but the fish hide today.

The river is warming, their time to get here is shortening.
And I can't stay in the heat.

A volunteer holds a chart: *590,000 so far this census.*
"Before the fish ladder, we hauled them up in buckets.
At least 19,000 one year. The herring brigades."

Henry and John, I can see you out here, pails in hand.

~

Our guide points out a skinny runway for American eels:
they land in a small metal box
after wiggling up.

The box is empty, but she notes: *13,200 eels in 2013.*

They swam 1,000 miles from the Sargasso Sea to mature here.

Dad would have loved this,
would have hauled buckets at ninety,
been furious at the pollution.

Emma's favorite sushi is Japanese eel—
in Kyoto she ate it for breakfast
with seaweed and raw eggs.

She sends me pictures of eel plates at dinners in Gifu City,
where cormorants tethered to rods
catch fish for tourists.

My daughter would be a fish counter if she were here.

~

At home, I watch videos of the fish via underwater cameras.
While I rest my swollen ankle on the ottoman,
they sleek-tail-it upstream nearby,
next to roads jammed with traffic.

Become a counter now—the screen reads—*in your own home—*
help save our water

I've counted thirty-two in ten seconds!—
I record what I've seen.

I tighten the Velcro snaps on my Tribute Wrap,
invented in Amsterdam,
its internal ribs a ladder
lifting my stubborn lymph
from ankle to knee.

And suddenly I think I see five American eels slither by,
grayish green and hard to spot.
But no, this is river grass.

No one has seen them spawn in the Sargasso Sea,
no one is sure how they find their way to American rivers,

but more eels will land in the metal box and someone will ease them
into the Upper Mystic Lake
where bass, cormorants, and gulls
will hunt them,
where black-crowned night herons
can eat them close to shore.

~

I remember the eels my father caught in New Jersey
and cooked on the grill, slimy
and curved like pool noodles.
I can barely look at Emma's plate when she eats eel,
even in their glassy young stage of life.
The Chinese catch them to sell to the Japanese.
If Dad were here, he'd try to save this river.

~

Henry addressed the river fish:

"Keep a stiff fin, then, and stem all the tides thou mayst meet."

~

When I worry about my daughters far from home,
                    I can count fish at my river.
When I worry about my foot swelling in the heat,
                    I can count fish in my living room.
When the stink of traffic and gas leaks on Mass. Avenue
                    makes me long for the ocean,
I can go to the Mystic Lakes and watch a blue heron.
                    I can uproot Oriental bittersweet.
                    I can prepare for the run back to the sea.

Notes

"The Battle of Menotomy": The bloodiest battle on April 19th, 1775 took place in this Massachusetts town now known as Arlington, not far from Lexington and Concord.

"The Father of Western Surgery in Tenth Century Andalusia Spain": Al-Zahrawai (936-1013) invented groundbreaking surgical techniques and instruments and wrote a thirty-volume medical and surgical encyclopedia that became a foundational text in Western medicine.

"Sea Otters, Missiles, Sardines": The Ainu are an ethnic group of indigenous peoples native to Northern Japan.

"Bruno Schulz from the Bardo": Schulz was a Polish Jewish fiction writer and visual artist. The poem's long-accepted version of Schulz's murder has recently been challenged, but not the fact that he was killed by the Nazis. Bennu is an asteroid on a possible collision course with Earth.

"Lines by Wisława Szymborska Rearranged as Elegy": The lines appear as translated by Stanisław Barańczk and Clare Cavanagh from multiple poems, with no consecutive lines from any poem.

Acknowledgments

My deep thanks to Steven Cramer and Joyce Peseroff, my gifted first readers, and to Bob and Ilona Bell, Danny Lawless, Steven Ratiner, and Kevin Prufer, who read these poems and honored me with their wise insights and support.

My gratitude to the editors of the publications in which these poems first appeared:

AGNI: "That Alley of Our Childhood," "Aesop's Crows"

The American Journal of Poetry: "At Risk," "Local Diner at 5 AM"

Crab Orchard Review: "Seeding the Flowerbed"

Ecotone: "Special Delivery"

The Louisville Review: "Lines by Wisława Szymborska Rearranged as Elegy," "When Syrinx Turns into a Lilac Bush"

Massachusetts Review: "Thoughts and Prayers," "The Second Time"

Memorious: "Forced Labor"

On the Seawall: "Urban River Run," "Noontime," "Junk Moon," "The Nine Children of Marianna Gluza," "Ode to Teased Hair"

Passengers Journal: "Isotopes," "The Season of Our Sundering"

Plume: "It Happened All the Time," "Postscript," "Sea Otters, Missiles, Sardines," "Bruno Schulz from the Bardo," "The Cycle," "To the Young Protestants on the Steps of the Catholic Cemetery in Bielsko on All Souls' Day"

Plume Anthology 7: "Stefania Takes the Ellis Island Literacy Test, Reading Bible Passages in Her Native Language"

Poems 2Go: "Postscript," reprinted

Poet Lore: "Sometimes, the Moon"

Red Letter Poems Project: "That Alley of Our Childhood" and "The Season of Our Sundering," reprinted; "Pythagoras Said the Soul of Homer Moved into a Peacock," "The Battle of Menotomy," "Cupid Peruses *The Times,*" "Metaphysics of the Seahorse"

Slate: "Ghazal of the Goats"

Sugar House Review: "The Man in the Hat," "San Pasqual," "Lunar Eclipse, Waterville Valley," "Bird's Nest with Ribbon"

In Polish Translation:

Fraza (University of Rzeszów): "It Happened All the Time," "Forced Labor," "Two Potatoes and a Dog, 1939," "Postscript," and "The Second Time," translated by Joanna Banach; "That Alley of Our Childhood," translated by Ewa Hryniewicz-Yarbrough.

Peace, Poetry & Policy: *An International Anthology:* "A Garden and a Street" and "Sea Otters, Missiles, Sardines" in English and Polish, translated by Joanna Banach.

Richard Snyder Publication Series

This book is the 27th in a series honoring the memory of Richard Snyder (1925-1986), poet, fiction writer, playwright, and longtime professor of English at Ashland University where he and Robert McGovern founded the Ashland Poetry Press in 1969. In selecting the manuscript for this award, editors kept in mind Snyder's tenacious dedication to craftsmanship and thematic integrity.

Chuck Carlise, Series Editor, selected finalists for the 2023 contest. Final judge was Mark Doty.

Snyder Award winners:

1997: Wendy Battin for *Little Apocalypse*
1998: David Ray for *Demons in the Diner*
1999: Philip Brady for *Weal*
2000: Jan Lee Ande for *Instructions for Walking on Water*
2001: Corrine Clegg Hales for *Separate Escapes*
2002: Carol Barrett for *Calling in the Bones*
2003: Vern Rutsala for *The Moment's Equation*
2004: Christine Gelineau for *Remorseless Loyalty*
2005: Benjamin S. Grossberg for *Underwater Lengths in a Single Breath*
2006: Lorna Knowles Blake for *Permanent Address*
2007: Helen Pruitt Wallace for *Shimming the Glass House*
2008: Marc J. Sheehan for *Vengeful Hymns*
2009: Jason Schneiderman for *Striking Surface*
2010: Mary Makofske for *Traction*
2011: Gabriel Spera for *The Rigid Body*
2012: Robin Davidson for *Luminous Other*
2013: J. David Cummings for *Tancho*
2014: Anna George Meek for *The Genome Rhapsodies*
2015: Daneen Wardrop for *Life As It*
2016: Pamela Sutton for *Burning My Birth Certificate*
2017: Michael S. Moos for *The Idea of the Garden*

2018: Barbara Ungar for *Save Our Ship*
2019: Laura Donnelly for *Midwest Gothic*
2020: Peter Grandbois for *Last Night I Aged a Hundred Years*
2021: Margaret Mackinnon for *Afternoon in Cartago*
2022: Bruce Bond for *Vault*
2023: Teresa Cader for *AT RISK*